All the Way Home
Jane Clarke

smith|doorstop

Published 2019 by
Smith|Doorstop Books
The Poetry Business
Campo House
54 Campo Lane
Sheffield S1 2EG

ISBN 978-1-912196-68-5

Designed and Typeset by Utter
Printed by Biddles Books
Cover Image: © The Patricia Aubrey Collection / Mary Evans

Smith|Doorstop Books are a member of Inpress:
www.inpressbooks.co.uk. Distributed by NBN International, Airport
Business Centre, 10 Thornbury Road Plymouth PL6 7PP

The Poetry Business gratefully acknowledges the support
of Arts Council England.

Supported by
ARTS COUNCIL
ENGLAND

Contents

*It will all be over one day, and
what a day it will be, won't it?*

Albert Auerbach (1894 – 1918)

Foreword

In April 2017 the Mary Evans Picture Library invited Jane Clarke to write a sequence of poems in response to the Auerbach family archive belonging to Patricia Aubrey and represented by the library. Consisting of family photos, documents and other items, the collection offers a unique insight into how the First World War affected the members of one family, in particular Patricia's uncle, Albert Auerbach, who died in action in September 1918, and her Aunt Lucy, who survived the war and lived on into the early 1970s.

Albert Auerbach and his elder sister Lucy were close and, alongside the photos, Albert's letters to Lucy from his overseas postings have been a particular source of inspiration for Jane, with their insight into the minutiae of a soldier's daily life.

Aged twenty, Albert joined up on 1st September 1914, the very first day of the war, as a private in the 20th Battalion, Royal Fusiliers. On 20th July 1915 he received his commission as 2nd Lieutenant in the 1st London Regiment. Albert's first posting was to Gallipoli in November 1915, where he was involved in the evacuation of Suvla Bay and Cape Helles. After a time in Egypt he was posted to France, from where he was invalided home with shell shock and dysentery on 3rd December 1916. He spent some time in hospital, but returned to France on 20th June 1918. He was killed by a shell at Bouchavesnes, Péronne, on the Somme, in the early morning of 1st September 1918, exactly four years to the day of his joining up.

During the war Lucy worked at the War Office in London, but occasionally travelled to the Worcestershire village of Madresfield, near Malvern, to help with agricultural and dairy work. A gifted pianist, she made her living after the war as a piano teacher.

Albert was posthumously awarded the Military Cross, presented to his mother at Wellington Barracks, London, on 10th July 1919. His sister Lucy made her own personal pilgrimage to the Somme area in September 1920 to see where her brother had fought and died.

November 1918, a time of relief, happiness and peace for some, was a time of tragic bereavement for the Auerbach family, who had lost their eldest son just as the war was coming to an end.

Gill Stoker, Mary Evans Picture Library, April 2019

September

The week before he left for France
we leaned a ladder into the apple trees,

picked Cox's Orange Pippins,
Newton Wonders, Brownlee's Russets,

laid them one by one
on dusty floorboards in the attic,

then planted hyacinths and amaryllis for spring.
We sat out after dinner

and talked of how we loved
this time of year,

when hollyhocks are past their best
but still stand tall

in copper, pink and cream,
beside clematis and the last of the sweet pea.

Mortal Wound

The gunner recites his village
easing in for the night –

horse chestnut trees circling the green,
children on swings,

their mother's shout, *come in
out of that or the púca will catch you,*

a couple sitting close on a bench,
oblivious to everything,

someone calls *quiet* for the weather forecast,
no stars to be seen,

but sure as a loaf on the back of the stove,
the moon slowly on the rise.

The Game, St. Stephen's Day 1916

*from an eyewitness account by Fr. Browne,
chaplain to the Irish Guards.*

The goal posts were blown
to match sticks –

seven men wounded,
two defenders
and a keeper dead.

Still hot,
their bodies were stretchered
from the pitch.

Friends filled their places.
The ref blew the whistle again.

In the Dugout

To pass the time in the dugout, we play
the 'when all this is over' game.

In the beginning our plans were bold,
one chap keen to outdo the next.

Now it's *a drink in the local,*
Sunday dinner with all the trimmings,

to walk in the Malverns,
waltz with my wife in the kitchen,

hold my mother's hand,
watch my children sleep,

wishes distilled to the final drop
like Scotch in a copper still.

The Arch

Not tudor or corbel,
lancet or gothic,

not burdened by a bridge
or chastened by a church,

but hewn from rough limestone blocks,
wedged flank to flank by peasant masons,

it stands at the end of the avenue
in chestnut tree shade.

It has sent off scoundrels,
barred bailiffs from entry,

welcomed carriages home.
It never sleeps on duty,

never refuses swallows a nest,
never tells stories better unsaid.

Years it watched the courtyard walls
crumble and fall, till it was left alone.

One day it will stop trying to hold
what can no longer be held.

After We're Gone

farmers will level this ground,
backfilling shell-holes and trenches,

picking coins, buttons, tin cups,
boot laces, shaving mugs, razors

from soil that has buried letters,
curses, men and horses.

They'll never know one of the lads
keeps celandine and meadowsweet

in a whiskey glass by his pallet,
another passes the time at the parapet

naming the flowers in his mother's garden;
foxgloves, peonies, lupins, heart's ease.

When I try to forget
the smell of burning flesh, I see

neighbours with pitchforks,
rakes and scythes

between hedges scented
by honeysuckle and wild rose.

Base Hospital, Boulogne

When the doctor got started
on sphagnum moss

he couldn't be stopped –
he spoke of old men, women and children

knee-deep in Clara Bog,
bending to hummocks of yellow, bronze and green,

picking out twigs and leaves,
beetles, dragonflies, frogs,

packing it wet into burlap sacks,
lifting them onto donkey carts.

He pointed to mounds of dressings
and rest pillows for splints and stumps.

There'd be many more buried, he said,
were it not for the barrel cells

that absorb sweat, soak up pus,
staunch pints of blood.

Pitch

Not easy to keep a balanced pitch,
one note blended to the other,

    impossible to prevent the losses

wrought by weather. Pressures
of heavy play cause the sound board to swell,

    stretching strings, building tension.

If I could open the lid, remove the panels,
I'd listen for the note that's wavering.

    I'd wield hammer and mute,

arrange the strings, align the intervals,
set the pins.

    I'd play Pachelbel's Canon for you;

there's sanctuary
in the same eight notes repeating,

    the bass line that anchors the melody,

giving answers to questions
the treble line tries to escape.

When All This is Over

we'll follow a path
    through silver birch and pine

listen for the shepherd
    whistling to her flock of pregnant ewes

look for grasses
    herbs trampled under their hooves

catch the scent
    of crushed chamomile lavender thyme

from the mossy mountainside
    drink the river's source

Milk

Tall as my hip, the gentlest creature
I've ever met, she waits by the manger
while I, on a three-legged stool,

tuck myself close to her belly,
my legs hugging the bucket tight.
I hold each udder between thumb

and first finger, then squeeze –
it takes time to find the flowing
movement that releases the milk.

Meanwhile my companion stands,
her warm teats filling my hands,
that have been so empty and cold.

The Axe

she ignores the welts   seeping blisters
        aches in her back

grips handle and haft
        lifts it back over her shoulder

and brings it forward
        to strike

by the end of the week
        she wields it as well as any man

not the strength of her arm
        but the arc of her swing

Bells

let's leave all the talk of war
      and walk this cobbled street

under balconies that flap yellow
      and pink with pillow-cases and sheets

let's take the shade that's given
      on our way uphill to the square

where dusty wax trees listen
      to church bells pealing

like children
      let loose from school

let's sip our café au lait
      at the foot of the tower

while the ringer
      grips the sally tight

lest the bells break free
      to toll a grief of their own

Refugee

No one knew how
she smuggled a piano,
wrapped in a blanket,

all the way from the city.
We didn't want trouble,
neighbours said we should burn it,

but if you saw how she touched it,
you'd know why we found
a hiding place in a distant shed.

Like everyone else,
she spent long days in the fields
but come the night

she'd be gone for hours at a time.
We didn't ask,
didn't want to know;

only sometimes we heard notes
carried, as if from the heavens,
by hard frost or on the wind.

Ling

A sprig of heather falling
from my sister's letter

carries me north
to the Cairngorms in August –

a sea of honey-scented ling,
purple flowers teeming with bees.

A shepherd told us
that at the time of creation

no plant would cover
the bare mountain slopes;

only heather, out of kindness,
offered its modest growth.

A brave little plant, he called it.
No matter how trampled

by rutting stags,
the woody branches spring back.

Priam of Troy

Poor as a peddler
    in a mule-drawn cart,
        he leaves his city at night –

bound for the camp across the plain,
    carrying gifts;
        the finest tunics,

robes, blankets, cloaks,
    woven from wool
        of young sheep and goats,

woven to warm,
    comfort, bind
        what is broken.

Bouchavesnes

Some men sing, some men chat,
all complain about the heat;

we've been digging since early
this morning, another twenty graves.

While we bend and lift,
wielding pickaxe, mattock, spade,

I think of Grandpa's advice
when digging potatoes –

wait till the vines have died down,
he'd say, be sure to dig gently

or you'll bruise the tubers that huddle
like hens' eggs under the mound.

Then let your shovel lift
seven, eight, nine, into the light.

News

At half-past two I give up
trying to sleep, find my way

to the window, creak open
reluctant shutters.

A few village lights
in the distance,

a sprinkling of stars –
hand-thrown seeds.

I stay at the window,
saving these moments.

Snow

began to fall before dawn,
blown horizontal in easterly winds
from across the hill. By evening
it lies deep in banks and drifts;

hedges become whitewashed walls,
barrels turn into haystacks,
the wood pile disappears.
I could almost believe

that we haven't received
your mud-caked kit, breeches ripped
from ankle to hip, bloodied tunic,
your helmet, slightly dinged,

and the watch you won at school.
I could believe you'll be with us
for dinner, having walked in your trench boots,
all the way home through the snow.

The Pianist

she plays
into silence

a harbour
at dusk

makes wind-ripples
over the surface

until her fingers
begin to insist

hail stones
on the slipway

she dives
like a cormorant dives

leaves only
a circle of bubbles

we listen
for where she'll emerge

taking
our breath

she dives
again and again

returns us
to quietness

Pruning

never forget the one
who showed you

when to whet
the secateurs

how to keep
broadest angles

guiding
scaffold limbs

where to lance
the lowest branches

why to cut
above the buds on apple boughs

the one who taught you
to trust in sap

it'll rise again
in battered stems

Rowan

When grief
like a river

is set
to burst its banks

the rowan
has already lost

its berries
and leaves;

it sways
in the wind,

steadies
and sways.

Image captions and copyright

Front cover
Albert Auerbach (left) and fellow-member of the Royal Fusiliers relaxing during a training exercise in the UK, summer 1915.

Frontispiece
Albert Auerbach in Northern France, 1918.

Foreword (p7)
Young army recruits marching, including Albert Auerbach, Epsom, Surrey, autumn 1914.

September (p9)
Albert Auerbach (right) and other soldiers leaving by train, 1918.

In the Dugout (p13)
Albert Auerbach in Northern France, 1918.

Base Hospital, Boulogne (p17)
Collecting sphagnum moss for dressings, 1917.
© Illustrated London News Ltd/Mary Evans

Milk (p21)
Lucy Auerbach with Midget, the Jersey cow, Madresfield, Worcestershire, 1915.

Refugee (p25)
Belgian refugee in a street, guarding her possessions, 1914.
© Süddeutsche Zeitung / Mary Evans

Bouchavesnes (p29)
Albert Auerbach (centre back) and fellow-recruits, Epsom, Surrey, autumn 1914.

The Pianist (p33)
Lucy Auerbach visiting a former battlefield near Bouchavesnes, Somme, 1920.

This page
Headstones of Albert Auerbach and others, Sailly-Saillisel Military Cemetery, Northern France, April 1930.

Acknowledgements

Thanks to the editors of the anthologies, journals and blogs in which several of these poems first appeared: *Poetry Ireland Review, New Hibernia Review, The Stony Thursday Book, One, The High Window* and the Mary Evans Picture Library Poems and Pictures Blog. Thanks also to The Poetry Programme and Arena, RTE Radio One, where several of these poems were first broadcast.

Many thanks to Gill Stoker in the Mary Evans Picture Library who had the original idea for this publication and worked tirelessly to bring it to fruition. I am very grateful to Patricia Aubrey for her generous engagement with my response to her family's story.

My gratitude to the colleagues and friends who helped shape the sequence; Rosamund Taylor, Eithne Hand, Jess Traynor, Catherine Phil MacCarthy, Stuart Pickford, Éadaoin Ní Chléirigh and Penelope Shuttle. Many thanks to Ann and Peter Sansom, Eleanor Holmshaw, Keith Lauchlan and all at Smith|Doorstop Books.

I wish to gratefully acknowledge the award of a literature bursary by the Arts Council of Ireland in 2017. My gratitude also to Isobel O'Duffy and Andrew Clarke for their guidance and support every step of the way.